WRITING FASTER FOR THE WIN

SECOND EDITION

L.A. WITT

Copyright Information

Writing Faster For the Win

Second Edition

Copyright © 2015, 2023 L.A. Witt

First edition published as Writing Faster FTW

Copyright © 2015 L.A. Witt

Cover Art by Lori Witt

Paperback ISBN: 978-1-64230-165-6

❀ Created with Vellum

ABOUT WRITING FASTER FOR THE WIN

Frustrated with your writing output? Looking for ways to get the words moving?

L.A. Witt has written and published nearly 200 romance novels, novellas, and short stories since 2008, and in *Writing Faster For The Win*, she shares some techniques for getting the words out of your head and onto the screen faster than before.

Whether it's shaking off insecurities and self-doubt, streamlining the research process, or writing out of sequence, you may just find the advice you've been looking for.

To every writer who's ever given me wings.

Also, thank you to author Erica Cameron for beta reading this book.

INTRODUCTION

WHAT THIS BOOK IS, AND WHAT THIS BOOK ISN'T.

If you've picked up this book, chances are you're trying to find ways to increase your writing output. And since I'm the one writing this book, just who in the world do I think I am?

Basically, I'm a writer who writes fast. I've been writing full-time since the end of 2008. Every writer has their strengths and weaknesses, and if there's one aspect of this craft that I know, it's how to get words out of my skull and onto my screen at a steady clip. I started writing at speed during NaNoWriMo 2008, and pretty much haven't stopped. Since then, I've written or co-written close to 150 novels, around 45 novellas and 20 short stories.

My output is roughly 80,000 words a month, give or take 20-30K depending on what else is going on in my life, and I write between 750,000 and 1,000,000 words per year (not counting my co-writers' contributions to our joint works – I only count what I've written).

As such, I get a lot of questions about it, mostly "How?"

So, I decided to write a short book with some tips for writing faster. There's also some general commentary on not driving yourself up a wall (and stalling out) with your story because in a lot of situations, the key to writing fast is knocking over some mental obstacles in your writing technique. i.e., spending less time banging your head against the keyboard and more time tapping your fingers on it.

For some, upping your speed is a matter of technique. For others, it's a mindset—getting past insecurities and shaking off bad (if well-intentioned) advice. So, sections of this book will deal with both angles. Feel free to skip what doesn't apply to you. Also, any time you run into advice, tips, or techniques that don't work for you, feel free to skip those too.

I also want to preface this book by saying that writing fast does not equate to writing better. I *can't* write slow because I get frustrated and impatient. Other writers are solid and consistent at a few hundred words a day, and that's a comfortable pace for them. I say this because writers seem to fall into two camps—those who write fast, and those who write slow. There are always people who have something negative to say about one camp or the other. The slow writers are lazy. The fast writers don't care about quality. The slow writers are pretentious. The fast writers just churn out garbage.

All of which, I believe, is nonsense. I've read garbage written by both fast and slow writers, and gold written by both fast and slow writers. Laziness certainly has no speed limit. Fast writers can burn out, but so can slow ones. Slow writers can produce very little, but fast writers can certainly be non-productive too. For that matter, a slow writer who produces 500 words a day will still write more than the fast writer who writes a novel in two weeks, but burns out and stops writing for a year.

The bottom line is that every writer has their comfortable pace, and there is no shame in writing fast *or* slow. This book is not a judgment of slow writers, nor is it praise of fast writers—it is simply a tool for those who would like to increase their productivity for whatever reason, based on things I've done and learned in my own career.

If you're reading this book because you've been led to believe that writing slow makes you a bad writer, you've been led wrong. Slow is absolutely okay. Is there anything wrong with trying to up your productivity? Certainly not. Will increasing your speed hurt your quality? That's up to you—personally, I believe that when you write your 5,000th word of the day, you still know how to write just as well as you did when you wrote your hundredth word of the day. But if you find that writing fast wears you down, and fatigue hinders your quality, then there is no shame in reining your quota back until you find the amount you can produce, with consistent quality, every time you sit down to write.

Side note: When we're talking about word counts and quotas, it goes without saying that you're still writing *good words*. Sure, it's a first draft, and it'll need editing. They all do. That's okay. But don't throw garbage on the page to fill your quota. More on that later.

Also, I'd like to make it clear before we get started that when I talk about my numbers (my quotas, hours spent writing each day, etc.), I'm using examples from my work to illustrate how I do things, but I don't want you to get discouraged by those numbers if yours are different. Please keep in mind that I am a full-time writer. Early in my career, my writing sessions were eight hours or more, sometimes twelve or even sixteen. These days, it's closer to five or six hours a day. That's just writing—no admin, marketing, editing, etc., all of which take up their own blocks of time. Another writer's sessions might be an hour or two. That's going to have an impact on how many words happen during that time. We all have twenty-four hours in our day, but some of those hours are chewed up by other things, so each writer has to determine how much of the remaining time is available for writing. I don't come home from a day job and spend an hour writing before I have to help kids with homework. So take my numbers for what they are—examples from my experience—and apply the principles to your own numbers.

With all of that in mind, let's talk about what this book is *not*.

It will not magically turn you into a writing machine who can effortlessly knock out tens of thousands of words in a day. There are no incantations that will render you immune to burnout[1]. There will be no formulas for producing cookie-cutter books that need only a few details altered from one version to the next.

In this book, I will not be getting into artificial intelligence (AI), such as ChatGPT and other such apps, as I have not used them myself and have no intention of doing so.

As far as software goes, I tend to use Microsoft Word and Microsoft Excel (I'll get into how and why I use Excel later), but my methods do not require you to do the same. I know a lot of writers who use Scrivener, various open source programs, AlphaSmart devices, and even some who write longhand. You *do not* need to switch apps/methods in order to write more!

Essentially, this book is a collection of tips and techniques that I've applied over my career as an author. Some may be absolutely useless to you, while others may be exactly what you're looking for. Some of this information has appeared, in part or in full, on my blogs. Some of it is entirely new. Altogether, I hope it provides you with some methods for increasing your discipline and productivity.

Furthermore, none of the techniques I offer must be followed to the letter. While I recommend trying them as they're written, never ever be afraid to tailor something to your own needs. The purpose of this book—as with any writing book—is to give you information to help you on your writing journey, not create an army of writing clones who do everything exactly as I do. Though that would be kind of cool. I mean, imagine if I had a basement full of me-clones, writing just like I do. The coffee budget might get out of hand, though.

Anyway. Moving on...

I'm not going to tell you how to type faster. In fact, the idea is not so much to write *faster*, but to write *more*. To get the most out of every writing session.

Many of the things I'm going to discuss are, more than anything, about changing your mindset with regard to writing. Getting past insecurities, jealously guarding your writing time and space, and removing obstacles—mental and otherwise—that hinder your ability to write. Why are those in a book about writing faster? Because experience has shown that those seeking methods of increasing writing speed are often struggling to write at all. It won't do you any good to prepare for the Indy 500 if you're still worried about when to push in the clutch, so I'm including chapters on optimizing your writing sessions and adjusting your mindset. Once you're over those hurdles, improving your speed will be a piece of cake.

So with that said, you'll find a lot of general writing tips in here—ranging from discussing writing spaces to outlining techniques—because those things influence the discipline required to increase your productivity. Nothing I say in this book will do you any good without discipline, so I've included a few sections that may be useful whether or not you're trying to increase your output.

You will probably notice that I frequently mention that it's okay to do things differently, to reject my advice completely, and that there is no one way to do anything. The reason for this is that I've read a lot of the same writing books that you've probably read, and I get seriously Hulk-smash annoyed when I'm told that my way is wrong based solely on the evidence that it doesn't work for the author of that particular book. I spent too many of my formative writing years being afraid to reject advice that didn't work for me. I wasted absurd amounts of time and energy getting frustrated over techniques that were *The One & Only True Way*™, only to have someone come along and say, "Dude, no, you totally don't have to do it that way." I now know that such rejection doesn't mean that the advice isn't sound—it simply means that it doesn't work *for me*.

Which means that now is probably a good time to break out a thing you'll see throughout the book:

Things I learned the hard way so you don't have to: *If it works, it works, even if someone else loudly insists it doesn't work.*

Don't waste your energy shoehorning yourself into someone else's method. Writing advice is a buffet—take what you want and leave the rest. Just don't hog the tater tot casserole or we're taking this out to the parking lot.

Moving on...

Many of the tips in this book will assume that you're an outliner. If you are not an outliner, I still recommend that you read and digest each section. Some things may be adaptable for the non-outliner. For example, Marie Sexton,

an extremely amazing author who you all need to be reading, doesn't outline, but writes out of sequence, so a
"pantser" (aka, someone who writes by the seat of their
pants instead of outlining) can certainly benefit from the
chapters about out-of-sequence writing.

There will also be pointers and explanations of techniques that don't necessarily relate directly to improved
speed, but are the foundation of another technique that is.
For example, when you get to the chapter on bite-sized writing, you'll understand why I spent time explaining out-of-
sequence writing, word count tracking, and outlining.

Also, throughout, I will mention authors who have been
influential to me, and at the end of the book, list their
websites and a few examples of their work, along with
recommended reading for writers and other links you may
find useful.

Remember that there is no one right way to write. If
someone tells you that you must do something a certain
way, they're telling you that *they* must do it a certain way.
Over the thirty-plus years I've been studying the craft of
writing, I have been told that I *must* outline, must never
outline, must follow an outline completely without ever
deviating, must never edit as I go, should absolutely edit as I
go, must keep markets and publishing in mind before I even
begin, must not think about publishing until I'm finished,
etc.

In the end, writing is about figuring out what works for
you. If you must write chronologically without ever looking
back at what you've written until the manuscript is finished
and has sat in a drawer for six months, then do so. If you
prefer to jump all over the place, edit as you go, and give the
manuscript an edit only after you've had a celebratory
round of miniature golf, then go forth. If you have to write

on red construction paper while dangling upside down over a shark tank, just make sure you don't dangle so long that you pass out.

Basically, the techniques in this book boil down to:

1. **Time management.** Spend your writing time actually writing, rather than fighting with a flawed outline or over-planning.
2. **Balance**. Have a plan, but don't write it in blood.
3. **Maintaining momentum**. Don't stall out because you had to stop and look up a minor detail.

In the coming chapters, I'll explain how I do those things, and how you can adapt your current techniques to get more out of the time you spend writing. Go forth with an open mind. Hopefully some of these techniques can help you get as much written as possible during the time you have available.

With that out of the way, ONWARD!

PART 1

SPACE & TIME

THIS SPACE IS YOUR SPACE

FINDING & DEFENDING YOUR WRITING SPACE

Why in the world is there a chapter on writing spaces in a book about writing faster? Quite frankly, because it can make all the difference in the world when it comes to productivity. So let's take a minute and talk about where you're spending your writing sessions.

As with pretty much everything, there is no one size fits all writing space. I prefer an office with my two cats sleeping on my desk, music playing, and no television within a ten-mile radius. I know writers who use kitchen tables, couches, coffee shops, sun rooms, or wherever they can set a laptop. I even know a few who write while watching TV, which is further proof that every writer is different. In fact, the version of me who wrote the first edition of this book would lose her mind if she tried to write in the vicinity of a TV, whereas now I can write with a TV on in the room. I can even sort of follow what's going on, or I can tune it out completely. We are fluid and adaptable creatures, and what is an absolute dealbreaker now might not be one later on down the line.

But that doesn't mean it's *not* a dealbreaker *right now*. If the TV is a serious distraction for you, that doesn't mean you need to adapt and get used to it, and you're not being a diva or a princess by saying, "Hey, I can't work with this nearby." Change the environment as much as you realistically can. Move to a different space if that's possible. If there's no one else around, turn off the TV. If you have absolutely no choice but to have the TV within earshot and you have no way to blot out the sound or light, give yourself a little grace. Try writing a paragraph, or even a couple of sentences, and commit to writing more later once the distraction is no longer present. Don't try to force yourself to knuckle through if it's really screwing with your ability to focus.

As much as you are realistically able, though, reduce the distractions. You know what distracts and annoys you. Set up or select your writing space to minimize those things as best you can.

Things to consider:

- **Noise** – Music or no music? Is there a noise that bothers you? Can you get away from or change troublesome noise? Is there *enough* noise?
- **Lighting** – Is it bright enough? Is it dark enough? Are there any flickering lights nearby that might bother you? If you're prone to headaches or migraines, is the lightning going to aggravate that?
- **Comfort/Ergonomics** – Does your writing surface have proper support for your

wrists/arms without cutting off circulation? If you write longhand, are your pens the kind you can grip comfortably? Is your chair supportive and comfortable?

- **People** – Do you need to be completely alone? Are there people around who you can ignore? People you *can't* ignore?

Take some serious time getting your space set up. Carefully select furniture— one piece of valuable advice I've been given over the years is to spend your money not on a desk, but on a chair. Your neck and back will thank you.

If you can, let people around you know that this is your space—either all the time, or for your designated writing sessions—and that you're not to be disturbed[1]. If you prefer music, have your playlists ready before you sit down to write.

Things I learned the hard way so you don't have to: *Endlessly fiddling with a playlist is not writing.*

You get the idea. The reason I bring up all of these things is that any one of them can put a serious dent in your productivity. A sore back. Headaches from bad lighting. Distractions. When you sit down to write, you need to be comfortable and ready to get in the zone. How you accomplish that is up to you. I've spoken to writers who come to their desk dressed the way they would go to the office for a day job—business casual, shirt and tie, whatever. Being dressed for work puts them in the mindset to work.

Me? Pajamas, yo. I hated business casual when I had a

day job, and I hate it now. I dress for comfort. And besides, it's hard not to feel inspired when you're wearing Totoro slippers.

Whatever floats your writing boat.

Also, even though you may have a designated space for writing, don't hesitate to pick up and move once in a while. About every week or so, I start getting some wicked cabin fever, and my office starts closing in around me. When that happens, I'll go write in a restaurant, on a beach, in the library, or even on my back porch or living room. Some sort of change of scenery—it works wonders, especially if I'm having a Don't Wanna day.

So now you have a place to write. You have your coffee, your music, your Totoro slippers, your research material close at hand, and no distractions.

But do you have enough pens?

Is the air conditioner buzzing?

Could those birds outside chirp *any* louder?

Is the cat snoring?

Did you clean the bathroom?

See where I'm going with this?

You could write in a sensory deprivation chamber with a laptop battery that lasts forever and an endless fountain of coffee at your disposal while a staff of ninjas caters to every potential chore and crisis, and there will always be a potential distraction. This, my friend, is where we begin to separate the wheat from the chaff. The writers who are going to write no matter what, and the procrastinators who will find any reason not to. When something disrupts your environment, this is where you have three choices:

1. ***Surrender* to the disruption.** Cancel your

writing session and try again later. I can't work in these conditions.

2. ***Fix* the disruption**. Change your location. Correct the problem. Feed the whining cat. Shut off the rattling air conditioner. Tell the aliens this is not a convenient time for an abduction.

3. ***Ignore* the disruption.** It is what it is— write anyway. Your mother-in-law is going to be mad at you no matter what, so you might as well finish this scene.

Of course, #2 and #3 aren't always options. Stuff happens, and that's okay. But don't let #1 be your default setting. Remember, your Muse is not a house of cards. The slightest breeze will not send it toppling.

Ultimately, this comes down to discipline. While we all certainly have our ideal setting and environment for writing, that ideal isn't always possible, and in those instances, the writer must push through.

I know of what I speak. I have the most amazing home office, but I have written in an emergency room with an IV hooked to my arm (twice), lying on the floor of a cargo jet at 30,000 feet, in airports, food courts, doctor's offices, buses, trains, hotel rooms, the lobby of a funeral home[2], a taxi cab, on ferry boats...

You get the idea.

Sometimes, the environment is not great, but the words can still happen. If you want to increase your productivity, you must be ready to push through circumstances that are not ideal.

So, before you read any further, write down the

following and fasten it somewhere in your writing space so
you can see it:

> Don't make excuses—make words.

And now... you're ready to write.

THIS TIME IS YOUR TIME

FINDING & DEFENDING YOUR WRITING TIME

Every October, with NaNoWriMo looming on the horizon, the inevitable discussions about making time, having time, etc., begin all over the intertubes. And every year, it's the same:

"I would do NaNo, but I don't have time."
"I don't have time to write every day."
"I wish I had as much free time as you do."

So, I've decided it's time for some tough love.

Now, there are people who have legitimate things occupying their time and keeping them from devoting as much time to writing as they'd like. When you're working 12 hours a day, 6 days a week, then you do have less available time than someone who works part-time or not at all. When you have a full-time courseload at a university and have loads of studying to do, you're going to have less time available than someone who doesn't. It's simple math. There's twenty-four hours in everyone's day, but some people have more of that time carved out for non-negotiable things. 'Tis a fact of life.

BUT.

If you're reading this book, then I assume you're looking for ways to increase your productivity. With that in mind, I've noticed some trends on social media when people discuss their limited time.

If you can carve an hour a day out of your schedule, then you have time to write. Even if it's fifteen minutes here, ten there, whatever, every little bit adds up. Now, I know some of us are the types of writers who need a big block of uninterrupted time to write, rather than doing it in tiny increments. But if that's what you have, then use it.

Take advantage of every opportunity. Waiting rooms. Lunch hours. Setting your alarm an hour early in the morning or staying up an extra hour at night.

Write anywhere and everywhere. Don't play the precious snowflake who has to sit at a specific place in order to write. If your life allows you to have such a place and spend time there, then by all means, use it. However, if you have to take advantage of every sliver of time you can find, don't be choosy about the where any more than the when. As I've said before, I have literally written in airports, doctor's offices, banquets, and airplanes. I have *on two separate occasions* had emergency room staff attach an IV to my right arm instead of my left so that I could continue writing (I'm left-handed).

"But...but...but..." I hear you say.

But, nothing. The times and places are out there, and if you want to write, you'll find the time and place to do so.

If you...

- Can quote last night's *Walking Dead* episode almost verbatim,
- Can give at least three reasons why the judges on *The Voice* are full of crap,

- Know the life stories, musical strengths and weaknesses, and personality quirks of every finalist on *American Idol* or whatever the kids are watching these days,
- Have an active and thriving account on the latest social media game,
- Post lengthy, daily blog entries about wanting to write, planning to write, and thinking about writing,
- Engage in political debates on social media,
- Frequently have quiz results posted on your Facebook wall,
- Create fan videos to post on YouTube, TikTok, etc.,
- Post on social media about the discipline, dedication, and time commitment required to be a novelist,
- Tweet or post on Facebook every few minutes to express your fury or happiness about the latest play of your favorite professional sports team...

...then you have time to write.

So whether it's social media, television, or whatever other distraction is out there, the truth remains the same:

**If you want to write,
don't bare your neck to time vampires.**

And while we're on the subject....

SOCIAL MEDIA

THE BIGGEST TIME VAMPIRE OF THEM ALL

All right, y'all. It's *really* time for some tough love.

It's time to talk about the internet. Specifically, social media.

Once upon a time, a writer came to me and said she was frustrated that her productivity wasn't great. In the time it took most of her peers to write four, five, or six novels, she struggled to finish a novella.

"What am I doing wrong?" she asked.

I couldn't say for sure. She was a pretty fast writer, and she didn't have any major stressors in her life that were interfering with her ability to write. Her sales were good, her books were getting reviewed, and everything generally seemed okay. But for whatever reason, her productivity had tanked.

Later that day, I was scrolling through my Facebook newsfeed, and saw her name pop up. Then again. Then again. So I got curious, and went directly to her profile.

There, I found numerous posts made within the past twenty-four hours. Each time, she had linked to—and commented on—lengthy articles about various topics.

Sometimes there'd be a blog post with dozens, even hundreds of comments, and I'd find her name sprinkled throughout. On one post in particular, it took me nearly an hour to get through the post itself and skim over the comments.

And I got to thinking, if it took me that long to read the article and comments, how long did it take *her* to digest it all and come up with lengthy, thoughtful comments? *Several* lengthy, thoughtful comments, for that matter?

I checked out her Twitter feed, and found that she had tens of thousands of tweets, many of them part of debates and discussions on various topics. Tumblr, same thing.

So I pinged her on chat.

"I think I've figured out the problem."

She wasn't happy with the assessment, but she agreed to scale back her online time as an experiment. Sure enough, her writing speed picked up again.

The moral to the story here is not that you need to avoid the internet or stay off social media. Quite the contrary! The key here is moderation. The problem is that social media doesn't exactly lend itself to moderation. Between Twitter, Tumblr, Facebook, e-mail, Pinterest, YouTube, Instagram, and whatever other form of social media has been invented in the time it took me to type that sentence, the internet is a veritable cornucopia of distraction.

If you're serious about improving your productivity as a writer, take a good, honest look at how you spend your time when you're online. Ask yourself which corners of the internet are nothing more than time vampires. If need be, uninstall games, apps, even browsers from the device you use for your writing. Turn off alerts and e-mail notifications. For example, I have virtually no push notifications on my phone. I get notifications if someone sends me a text message. That's it. And there are literally two people who text me with any semblance of regularity. Otherwise, I don't get notifications until I actually log on to whatever social media site wants to notify me of something.

So, let's also talk about the blogs, debates, and discussions. Am I suggesting you can't get involved in debates and discussions? Of course not! In fact, I'm very active in political discussions and generally on social media. The key is to be vigilant of how much it eats into your writing time. Be mindful of how much energy things like online debates can suck out of you, and whether you want to use that energy to argue with avatars or work on your story.

And yes, I absolutely practice what I preach here. There are no games on my laptop. I closed my account on a site where I'd frequently get into long, cumbersome debates that were devouring my writing time. I do stay engaged on certain social media sites, but then I close the tab completely so I don't have notifications pinging and distracting me.

Instant message programs can become major time sucks, too. I used to have three separate chat clients, but have since uninstalled all but one. That remaining one only has a handful of contacts who are typically as busy as I am. In fact, I tend to keep most communication to email; then I have the option to respond when I have a moment rather than feeling like I must respond instantly to an IM.

You don't have to apologize for not appearing visible, or for not engaging people. Just because you're on your computer does not mean you're obligated to be available for chat. It's no different than if you're at a day job—if someone sends you a personal email or IM during working hours, it's expected that you're going to respond when you have a moment. Treat messages received during your writing time the same way.

You don't need to cancel all your accounts and disappear completely from the internet. Trust me—I still get in plenty of internet time, as do most writers I know! Just be aware of how much time you spend browsing, chatting, arguing, etc. The internet does not lend itself to discipline and moderation, but for the writer, those things are key, especially since we often work on the same machines we use for games and social media.

Recommendations:

- Set a timer or an alarm when you log onto a particular site. When that alarm dings, close the site and write X words before you can revisit it.
- Make social media a reward. After you've written X words, you can visit Facebook or Tumblr for half an hour.
- Close accounts that you don't need or want to use anymore.
- Stay off sites and out of communities that are toxic, excessively time-consuming, or require so much energy that you have nothing left for writing.

PART 2

IT'S ALL IN
YOUR HEAD

CHANGE YOUR MIND, CHANGE YOUR GAME

SILENCING YOUR INSECURITIES

The ability to write faster won't do any of us any good if we freeze up on first contact with the blinking cursor. And if you've ever stared down a blank document, eyeing that cursor like it's a venomous snake, I assure you—you're not alone.

Taking it upon yourself to write a story is an intimidating prospect. I mean, just what kind of cocky bastards are we, thinking that if we put pen to paper, someone will want to read the results? Who do we think we are?

Answer: We're a lot more likely to be read than people who never write anything at all.

And really, anything worth doing is bound to be scary. Writing definitely falls into that category. I know a lot of writers, and I honestly don't know a single one who doesn't still have at least some of the insecurities they had when they first started out.

Notice that I titled this chapter *Silencing* Your Insecurities rather than eliminating them. It would be awesome if I could tell you that there will come a time when you write and publish with full confidence and not a trace of insecurity. Maybe you will. If you're anything like the rest of us, though, those insecurities are stubborn. They stick around.

After all, seasoned performers still get stage fright. Professional athletes still get nervous before the big game.

One of the biggest confidence boosters for me was learning that other writers have insecurities too. Authors I greatly admire still get queasy when edits arrive. *Did my editor hate it? Do I have to rewrite the whole thing from scratch? Is this the one where they finally realize I'm a fraud and tell me to kick rocks?*

It's okay!

It's okay to be insecure. It's okay to be afraid of rejection or failure.

While we're on the subject, there's one question that seems to come up everywhere when you have people trying to learn a new craft. It's a question about methods and techniques, one that comes in many, many forms but still boils down to one simple question:

What if I do it wrong?

Well, what if you do?

In fact, you probably will. You're going to screw it up royally. You're going to butcher it, burn it, break it, bust it, and pretty much bungle it up something awful.

You will then learn from your mistakes, salvage what you can, and move on.

That's not to say the only way to learn is the hard way. You don't *have* to make *every* mistake to learn from them. Remember, some people exist to serve as a warning to others. Learn from *their* mistakes whenever possible.

What I'm addressing is the crippling fear of failure that keeps people from sticking their necks out. It scares them

SILENCING YOUR INSECURITIES

The ability to write faster won't do any of us any good if we freeze up on first contact with the blinking cursor. And if you've ever stared down a blank document, eyeing that cursor like it's a venomous snake, I assure you—you're not alone.

Taking it upon yourself to write a story is an intimidating prospect. I mean, just what kind of cocky bastards are we, thinking that if we put pen to paper, someone will want to read the results? Who do we think we are?

Answer: We're a lot more likely to be read than people who never write anything at all.

And really, anything worth doing is bound to be scary. Writing definitely falls into that category. I know a lot of writers, and I honestly don't know a single one who doesn't still have at least some of the insecurities they had when they first started out.

Notice that I titled this chapter *Silencing* Your Insecurities rather than eliminating them. It would be awesome if I could tell you that there will come a time when you write and publish with full confidence and not a trace of insecurity. Maybe you will. If you're anything like the rest of us, though, those insecurities are stubborn. They stick around.

After all, seasoned performers still get stage fright. Professional athletes still get nervous before the big game.

One of the biggest confidence boosters for me was learning that other writers have insecurities too. Authors I greatly admire still get queasy when edits arrive. *Did my editor hate it? Do I have to rewrite the whole thing from scratch? Is this the one where they finally realize I'm a fraud and tell me to kick rocks?*

It's okay!

It's okay to be insecure. It's okay to be afraid of rejection or failure.

While we're on the subject, there's one question that seems to come up everywhere when you have people trying to learn a new craft. It's a question about methods and techniques, one that comes in many, many forms but still boils down to one simple question:

What if I do it wrong?

Well, what if you do?

In fact, you probably will. You're going to screw it up royally. You're going to butcher it, burn it, break it, bust it, and pretty much bungle it up something awful.

You will then learn from your mistakes, salvage what you can, and move on.

That's not to say the only way to learn is the hard way. You don't *have* to make *every* mistake to learn from them. Remember, some people exist to serve as a warning to others. Learn from *their* mistakes whenever possible.

What I'm addressing is the crippling fear of failure that keeps people from sticking their necks out. It scares them out of taking risk, and it isn't just beginners, either. Sometimes it's experienced writers (or painters, or what have you) who *want* to push the envelope a bit, but are scared. They know all the rules, but how far can they bend those rules?

Is it okay to write in first person from multiple points-of-view (POV)?

Can I write from the POV of the opposite gender?

Can I use [overused trope], but combine it with [cliche'] and a dash of [something new] to make it fresh?

Can I have four completely unrelated story lines weave together in a startling way to make poignant comment about the human condition?

The answer is: Yes.

Will you succeed? Will you make it work? Will it be publishable? Hell if I know. But it'll stand a better chance of getting published than the blank pages currently sitting in your printer with no ink on them. You won't know until you try.

You have to take risks if you want to master a craft. Taking risks means screwing up. Show me someone who's never made a colossal mistake, and I'll show you someone who's never created a masterpiece.

If you don't try, you are 100% guaranteed to fail. If you do try, you may still fail, but any gambler will tell you that those odds are decidedly better than the other option. Sure, if you don't put any money on the table, you won't lose anything when the roulette wheel stops. But wouldn't you feel like a tool if you thought "Hmm, I should put money on Black 17", but you didn't put that five dollar chip down, and the wheel stopped on Black 17? (Don't laugh—that happened to me at a roulette table once.)

Anyway. You don't have much to lose by trying. What? You thought I was going to say you have *nothing* to lose?

Pfft. Anything worth gaining requires giving something up, even if it's just some sweat off your brow or a few hours at the keyboard. For a book? Some time, a few sleepless nights if you're like me, some toner, a little space on your hard drive. The book you write may be a tome of epic failure comparable to my own failtastic fantasy novel, which was worthy of nothing more than violent and judicious application of the "delete" key and paper shredder. If the book isn't a total loss, then maybe it can be salvaged with some more time, some more toner, and some more space. What has been written can always be rewritten.

But whether the book is salvageable or should be killed with cleansing fire, you will have learned something from it, even if it's something as simple as "that doesn't work." You will apply that knowledge to your next book. And the one after. And the one after that.

In short, writing—like any craft—is learned through trial and error. This means that in order to learn the craft, you have to have the balls to try things and the intestinal fortitude to err, err, and err again. So what if you do it wrong? As long as you learn from it, it's not failure, it's education.

Quoth Thomas Edison:

> *"I have not failed.*
> *I've just found 10,000 ways that won't work."*

And again:

> *"I am not discouraged, because every wrong attempt*
> *discarded is another step forward."*

While he's not my favorite historical figure, he does make some valid points here.

Basically, try not to spend too much time or energy worrying about screwing up. That effort is better spent screwing up and learning from it. And if you do screw it up? That's perfectly okay. If a story is screwed up, it can be edited. Even if it isn't salvageable, those words were *not* a waste of time. I wrote that horrible epic fantasy three times —130,000 words *per draft*—before ultimately trunking it forever. Although it was disappointing to let it go, not one of those 390,000 words was a waste. Why? Because from the first word to the 390,000th, I'd learned a tremendous amount. I wasn't the same writer anymore, and when I embarked on my next book, I did so with the knowledge and wisdom I'd gained from those three drafts.

Someday, I may go back and revisit that fantasy story, and write it now that I have a better understanding of the craft. But even if I never do, it's okay, because I wouldn't be the writer I am now without having gone through that long, frustrating rite of passage.

The trick is to overcome the fear of the blinking cursor enough to get the words going. Write like the wind. Finish that book. Write another one. Learn from each and every book you write—I'm almost 200 books into this, and I *still* learn from every book. I *still* write books that need major rewriting because I screwed up. But the more you do it, the more you know you can fix mistakes, you can finish books, and *you can do this*.

Your insecurities won't necessarily go away, but by writing through them, what you're saying to your insecurities is that you hear them, you're aware of them, but you're not going to let them stop you. And while they might stick around, they'll get quieter with time.

Now what happens when you've finished your book and start getting published?

First of all, congratulations!

Second of all, well...

Let's just be completely honest about this: If you publish your book, I can pretty much guarantee that someone, somewhere will hate it. There will be bad reviews. There is no pretending that a book will be universally loved. You will, at some point in your career, get the review that says "If I could give this book ZERO stars instead of one, I would."

If that makes you feel like it's not worthwhile, go log onto Goodreads right now. Look up your five favorite books, or maybe five of the classics. Now look at their one-star reviews.

See what I mean?

It's okay if some people hate your book. You're not writing for them. You're writing for the people who are going to connect with your characters and sit on the edge of their seat, burning through the pages to find out what's going to happen next. You're writing for the people who will auto-buy the sequel, watch your Twitter feed for news of upcoming books, and shyly approach you at conventions to tell you how much of an impact your book had on them.

**Don't be afraid of the people
who won't like your book.
Write for the people who *will*.**

C'MON, FOCUS!

Before moving on to actual techniques, there's one more thing we need to talk about—procrastination. Now, I could be the poster child for inability to focus. On a good day, I have the attention span of a cracked-out squirrel. And let's face it—writers are champions at finding things to do besides writing.

So let's just get this out of the way. Here's the cold hard honest brutal truth:

**Your book does not exist
until you've written it.**

Things that don't matter until your book exists:

- Your query letter.
- Your dedication.
- Your chosen font.
- Two spaces or one after a period.
- Cover art.
- Press releases.

- How to format your table of contents.
- Author photos.
- Translating it into foreign languages.
- How much each copy should cost.
- The back cover blurb.
- Interviews on websites, blogs, radio stations, etc.

That's not to say you shouldn't be thinking about the market for your book. It isn't to say you shouldn't have agents or publishers in mind. It is, however, to say that at this stage, your primary focus is writing your book. Bringing it into existence.

It's also not to say that I've never been guilty of any of this myself...

Things I learned the hard way so you don't have to: *Concentrating on things that won't matter until just before the book is ready to be published do not contribute to the book being written, and will in fact hinder the same.*

All of those things will be relevant in due time, but at this stage, your task—your *only* task—is to produce the book. Don't waste your time doing things that won't matter until you've completed that step!

PART 3

TOOLS, TECHNIQUES, & TRICKS

RESEARCH

Research is a tricky area. How much research do you need to do? How much time should you spend researching? How long is a piece of string?

First of all, certain books require more research than others. A contemporary romance set in your hometown with a character in a similar field as you will probably not require quite as much research as, say, an espionage novel set on the other side of a world in a period of history that you don't know very well[1]. You may still need to look up details for that contemporary, but you won't have to stop and check whether the character's boots should slip on or lace up, or if ballpoint pens existed.

That said, research can become a method of procrastination. Essentially, its own time vampire. If you're intimidated by your story—and that does happen—doing "just a little more research" is a perfectly legitimate and convenient excuse to not write it.

So how do you know when to quit? How much research is too much? There's no one-size-fits-all answer for that one,

I'm afraid. Not for any one book, and not for any one author.

Let's start with books that require *some* research, but deal with topics/settings with which you're already somewhat familiar. This is where I employ the "shoot first, ask questions later" policy. Start plotting, start writing, and when you reach something unfamiliar, *then* do the research.

For example if you're fairly familiar with the Mafia, you can start in on your story, but then you might reach a point where you don't know who in the gang would complete a certain task or fill a certain role. Rather than going and researching the entire hierarchy of the Mafia, you can dial in your research to find the exact piece of information you need to know.

Or maybe it's a small but important detail that you can go back and address later. I'll get into this more in the chapter on using square brackets, but as an example, if your characters are getting into a particular car, does it have bench or bucket seats? Is the shifter on the steering column or on the console? In many cases, those details won't matter —you aren't going to mention the shifter, so you don't need to know where it is or how it's configured. But what if your passenger reaches over and grabs the shifter? Now you need to know where it is, so by all means, go look it up.

What you didn't need to do was waste a ton of time memorizing the precise configuration of the vehicle and details that won't matter to your story. You don't need to know if the backseat has lap belts only or over-shoulder seat belts if no one gets in the backseat, and even then, it might not matter.

These are examples where you either know the subject well enough that you don't need to research it before writing, or where the subject is only important enough to look up the details that need to land on your page. Don't get caught up in wasting time by hunting down the exact color thread used to stitch the leather seats in a red Jaguar F-TYPE unless that detail matters to your story. Otherwise, you're going to end up with a binder full of notes, a head full of trivia, and a manuscript full of absolutely nothing because you never got around to writing it.

This method has one other bonus: it can help the writer avoid the pitfall of trying to wedge *every* tidbit of researched information into a book. Because that temptation is a strong one. This way, you're not going on for pages and pages and pages about information that isn't relevant to the story, and doesn't really add anything. You're not tempted to find *some* way to work in the color of the stitching just because you researched it and want to include it.

Now, what about if your story involves, for example, an era or a culture with which you're not intimately familiar? In that case, some pre-writing research is necessary. And sometimes, depending on the genre and topic, that research may take weeks, months, or even years. The trick here is to decide when you're familiar enough with the subject matter to write about it.

Remember:

Don't get so bogged down in researching it that you forget to write the story.

Sometimes, the story you want to write is found while you're researching. As the information crystallizes in your mind, characters and plots can make themselves known. But how do you get to that point without knowing what to research in the first place?

Well, presumably you have at least a vague direction

you want to take. Maybe you know you want to write something around the American Civil War, or you want to write about pirates. In that case, you start with that tidbit, and start researching broadly.

For example, I decided I wanted to write a book about Ancient Roman gladiators, and that I wanted to set my book in Pompeii a year before the volcanic eruption that destroyed the city. That's all I had at the very beginning. No characters. No plot. Just gladiators in Pompeii.

So, I started out reading everything I could find that pertained to Pompeii, gladiators, and Roman life around that time period. As I delved deeper into the research material, I kept picking up bits and pieces about the Rome's social classes and politics, and at some point, my premise came to me:

A gladiator being used as a pawn by a corrupt politician.

Now, my research scope had narrowed pretty considerably. The more my outline crystallized, the more that scope narrowed. When I found myself reading research material and thinking "Okay, I already know this..." I decided it was time to stop. I had absorbed enough of the material to start writing.

Was I suddenly an expert in Pompeiian gladiators and Roman society? Not a chance! But I knew enough to create my characters, establish their motivations and obstacles, outline the story, and start putting together scenes. If and when I ran into something I didn't know—and that happened a lot!—I could look it up, same as I described above.

From the decision to write a Roman book to developing the story idea itself to stopping my research, it all happened over the course of a week.

I started writing. As I did, the research continued to a

certain extent. For some things, I absolutely shot first and asked questions later. When a gladiator is getting water, what exactly does he drink with? A ladle? A cup? His hands? I needed to know in order to make the scene authentic, but it wasn't important enough to stop writing and go look it up right then.

Other things had to be researched immediately because they determined how the scene would play out. For example, when my gladiator was going to fight in the arena, I knew what type of gladiator he was (a threaex), but I had to stop and check what kind of gladiator he'd be paired with because that would determine what weapons, techniques, strengths, and weaknesses he'd be facing. Without knowing that, I couldn't proceed, but I only needed to research those two specific types of gladiator rather than *all* of them. (He was paired with a myrmillo, for the record.)

Let me state for the record that in no way do I believe that research should ever come second to writing faster. Not at all. The idea is not to cut corners, but rather to *minimize the number of things that will prevent you from writing or will stop you once you've started*. What I'm advocating here is keeping the process efficient while avoiding the "just a few more chapters..." pitfall, which results in years of research and no writing getting done. Absolutely do your research... just don't let the research grind your writing to a halt.

Recommendations:

- Do your research, but know when you've done enough.
- It's okay to shoot first and ask questions later if

you have a reasonable grasp on what you're
writing about.

- Researching after the fact can help you look up
  a few specific facts and details that you need,
  rather than hundreds of them that you don't.
- Don't sacrifice research for speed, but don't use
  research to procrastinate.

[BRACKETS] ARE YOUR [FRIENDS]

In the earlyish years of my career, author Aislinn Kerry introduced me to a technique that would come to save me ridiculous amounts of time. She introduced me to....brackets. Just benign little [square] [brackets] that are about to become your bestest buddy *ever*.

The way it works is this. Let's say you're writing a scene in which your character goes into a bar, and runs into three people he knows. They're not terribly important to the story, but he wouldn't just refer to them as "that dude" and "whatever his name is" and "yeah, him." He'd refer to them by name.

The problem is, you're on a roll. You're writing like the wind, you've got a plan in mind for this scene, and now your character has spotted his three friends named...

Uh...

What are their names?

At this point, who cares? You're writing your first draft. You're getting the scene out of your skull and onto your screen, and are those three names really worth losing your momentum?

Of course not. Thus, as my good friend taught me, you'd write the scene as follows:

> *I strode in through the bar's front door, pausing just long enough to wave at [name1], [name2], and [name3] before I hurried to meet John in the back.*

See? No loss of momentum. Later on, you can come back, do a search for brackets, and fill in missing information. I sometimes do this at the end of the writing session, but it's not unusual at all for me to wait until I've finished the entire manuscript.

You can use whatever marker you want here. Brackets, parentheses, asterisks, bubble comments, etc. You can also use different font colors or highlighting, but I've found those to be a little less efficient because I have to scroll through the document to find them. With brackets or similar such marks, I can just do a Ctrl+F and go straight to them. You can also do search and replace that way.

Let's say you have a similar situation as above, where there's a character who needs a name, but isn't so important that he needs a name right now. He appears multiple times throughout the story, always referred to as [name1]. When you decide later that he's got a name, simply find and replace all instances of [name1] with his name.

Also, you don't have to use [name]. I've been known to use [someone], [bartender], [ex-boyfriend], [jerk], [sergeant] ... you get the idea. All you need is a bracketed placeholder so you can move on with the scene, returning later to bestow a proper name on the poor sap.

Things I learned the hard way so you don't have

to: *For obvious reasons, make sure you don't have four different people named [name2].*

Characters aren't the only ones with names that might require enough thought to bring your progress to a standstill.

They agreed to meet that evening at [restaurant].
   He pulled up in a red [sports car].
   She'd been away on business for the last week or so, and just flew in from [city].

The usefulness of brackets doesn't end with placeholders for proper names. I'll sometimes use them to remind myself that I need to double check a detail, especially things that I may have mentioned elsewhere but can't remember off the top of my head (and don't want to lose momentum by looking up):

"We talked about this [last Thursday]."
   The secretary absently brushed a few strands of [blonde] hair behind her ear.

Or maybe I need to look something up or confirm a fact:
   A pair of Seattle cops rolled past on [make/model] motorcycles.
   The SEAL had a gleaming trident on the [left breast pocket] of his uniform.
   It had been [six] grueling years, but he finally had his doctorate.

The fact-checking brackets are especially nice when I'm co-writing, particularly if my co-author and I are writing real-time in a shared document (more on that later). If I'm writing, and I put something in brackets, my co-author can go look it up while I continue with the scene, or either of us can address it later.

Bottom line, it's all about *momentum*. Do you really want to lose your momentum over a relatively minor detail? I don't. When I don't want to stop and figure out exactly which type of wine my amateur connoisseur would pair with his meal, I just write "He grabbed a bottle of [wine] off the rack," and move on.

Or if my character is driving a distinctive sports car, brought to him by the unimportant-to-the-story-but-named valet at the party "[valet] *brought the bright red [model] around to the front.*" One of my recent military romances is full of "[rank] [name] *turned to [name2]...*" and plenty of "*She boarded the [C130?] cargo jet...*" because the story was just cruising along, and I didn't want to stop to figure out names, which cargo jets flew out of Okinawa, what rank this or that person would be, etc.

Then, when there's some downtime—after I've finished the scene, made the day's goal, finished the entire book, or what have you—I do a search for "[", and correct them all. It does sound a little time-consuming, but it's really not. One recent book had over 50 sets of brackets, and it took me about ten minutes to resolve all of them. Even if it does get tedious, which it can sometimes, I would much rather do the googling/crowdsourcing/etc. after the book is finished than stall out while writing it.

Please note this is not limited to single words. As an example, if I'm writing a scene where a character is coming to meet someone at their home, I might be on a roll and don't want to stop and figure out exactly what this house looks like. I probably have an idea of the basics—whether we're going into a trailer park or Beverly Hills—but the specifics mean stopping to both figure it out and write it out. But I really want to get to the conversation they're about to have.

So, I just write:

"They pulled up to the house. [more details here]"

Later, after I'd written out the conversation I was itching to write, I went back and added a paragraph or so of description. This also meant I wasn't in a hurry to go write something else, so I could give the setting the attention it deserved.

The point is, I didn't have to stop writing the scene to fill those in.

Recommendations:

- Use bracketed placeholders for names, model numbers, places, etc.
- Use brackets to denote facts and details that you need to either look up or double check.

YOU DON'T HAVE TO GO ALONE

ALPHA READERS, WORD WARS, & CO-WRITERS

Over the years, I've been told not to show people my work until it's good and polished. And to a degree, it makes sense. There's no point in sending it to a beta reader to be edited or critiqued until it's truly finished.

That said, sometimes what a writer needs is encouragement. Some positive feedback. A little "Oh, wow, I want to read more!" can make a world of difference if you're struggling or you feel like your book has gone off the rails.

This is where the alpha reader comes in.

Unlike a beta reader, the alpha gets the first draft, hot off the press and largely uncorrected. When I send something to an alpha, I'll give it a quick read to make sure there isn't some giant, glaring error, but otherwise, it goes as is. It's understood that, being a first draft, it'll have the odd typo, some messy bits, etc. That's okay!

Why on earth would you send your messy first draft to someone else? Because they're sending you their messy first draft too. What do you gain from reading theirs?

- The realization that the person reading your messy first draft writes messy first drafts too.
- Instant feedback to silence the doubt gremlins. If you're second-guessing your story, a "Send more now!" from your alpha reader can be just the kick you need to continue. (I have had more than one novel saved by an emphatic "MORE PLEASE!" when I was feeling discouraged)
- Instant feedback about problems before you're too deep into the book.

As I mentioned above, you can get instant feedback from your alphas. This can be beneficial in that you'll catch major errors before getting so deep into the book that it'll take a massive rewrite to fix it. However, this isn't a good thing for all writers. For some, any negativity or criticism at this stage will stop them dead in their tracks and kill their interest in the story. You and your alpha need to decide where you stand on this.

Remember that your alpha is not the same as your beta or your editor—this person is there to urge you on. For some alpha duos, relentless, brutal criticism is perfect. For others, the alpha is there for camaraderie and mutual enthusiasm. Know where you stand with your alpha, and don't ever hesitate to talk about the situation if it isn't working.

And while we're on the subject of things that can be incredibly beneficial or absolutely disastrous, let's talk about NaNoWriMo and word wars.

NaNoWriMo is short for National Novel Writing Month. Every November, there's a challenge to write 50,000 words in a month. Writers encourage each other, compete with each other, have write-ins where they all get together and write, and it's a ton of fun. My career literally began with NaNoWriMo in 2008, so I can't recommend it enough for writers who are trying to improve their speed, find their stride, or just need a little *oomph* to get the words flowing.

During NaNo, people frequently engage in word wars, and it's something you can do on a smaller scale during any time of the year. Word wars are competitions between individual writers to meet a certain quota (say, 1,000 words in an hour) or to see who can write the most during a designated period of time. If the idea of competition makes you break out in hives, don't feel like you're obligated to try this. Competitive writing brings with it a breed of pressure that seems to either get the words moving or send the writer running.

Also, if it *sounds* like a good idea, but putting it into practice brings your progress to a grinding halt... don't. It's okay to drop out of a word war.

If you *are* competitive and have a writing buddy who's game, do some speed challenges. See if you can both hit 500 words in half an hour. Aim for 1,000 words in an hour. First one to 2,000 words gets a $0.99 song gifted to them on iTunes. Whatever floats your boat, but if a little friendly competition gets your fingers moving on the keyboard, do it.

You can also recruit other people via social media. The #1k1hr hashtag floats around on Twitter, along with #amwriting, and you can easily find people who are down for a little competitive word sprint. You can also join an online writing community, such as Absolute Write.

Writing is largely a solitary pursuit, but gentle competition and daily word-swaps with alpha readers can add some camaraderie, companionship, and motivation that isn't there when you go it alone.

Recommendations:

- Recruit an alpha reader to exchange rough drafts for mutual encouragement.
- Sign up for NaNoWriMo in November to challenge yourself to write 50,000 words in a month.
- Try word wars and other forms of friendly competition to motivate yourself and others.

TWO HEADS ARE (SOMETIMES) BETTER THAN ONE

A CO-WRITING PRIMER

Word wars and alpha/beta readers aside, does the actual writing process itself have to be a solitary pursuit? As a matter of fact, it doesn't!

Let's talk about co-writing.

Over the past decade or so, I've co-written with a number of people. As of this edition, Cari Z and I have written and published eleven novels, two novellas, and a short story since 2016, plus one that's due out in the fall of 2023. Anna Zabo and I have been co-writing since 2021, and we're working on our third book. I've even done a threeway co-write with K.A. Merikan, which is a pseudonym for an author pair.

What does co-writing have to do with writing faster, though?

Well, quite frankly—because co-writing happens very quickly! Also, if you're able to have multiple projects going at the same time, it's entirely possible to have your co-writer working on their chapter while you're working on a solo project, which means progress is being made on two books simultaneously. I'm nearly always working on something with both Cari and Anna, which means while they're working on our co-written books and I'm working on a solo project, three books are moving forward. Believe me when I say that adds up.

So, how exactly does one go about co-writing?

I've done it two different ways—real-time and alternating chapters.

Alternating chapters is fairly self-explanatory. In the cases of both Anna and Cari, we each take one of the two POV characters, write up a bio, and go from there. We figure out a basic plot, decide if we're writing first or third person and past or present tense, and off we go.

The fun part here is that you're writing for your co-author first, so your goal is to write a chapter that entertains them, and rather than making them want to *read* farther, it makes them want to *write* farther. They have to know what happens next... so they're excited to write it! And it's also a lot of fun to get the chapter back and see what they did with your character, the situation, etc., how they amped up the tension, and now *you* need to know (and write) what happens next. It really is a blast, and the momentum can get rolling seriously fast!

The other method is real-time writing. First, open a joint, real-time document. In the past, I've used Google Drive for this, and we set up the document so we can both access and edit. One of us starts writing while the other watches the words appear. Then they type a symbol that is agreed upon as an indicator that the other writer can take over. Then that person writes for a while. Whenever I've done this, each writer usually does 300-500 words, but if one person really goes off on a tear, it can be 1,000 words or more.

Both writers leap frog for as long as they both feel like

writing, and the words add up at a *blistering* pace. If a co-writer and I fall into a good rhythm and have a long stretch of time to work, we can easily knock out 10,000-20,000 words in a single session.

It sounds quite intimidating, since you effectively have someone looking over your shoulder as you're typing. I wasn't so sure about letting a co-author see every typo I made, or watching me fiddle with a sentence until I got it right, but that performance anxiety goes away pretty fast when you realize *everybody* fumbles and stumbles. In fact, many times, the person who isn't writing will follow along and fix typos/misspellings, or quickly research/tweak minor details.

The best part? When you get stuck, there is someone *right there* whose head is already in the same story, and you can bounce ideas off each other, or turn it over to the other person and see what direction they take it. Those moments when you stall out and find yourself staring into space? Gone. Or at least reduced to brief conversations. Co-writing isn't for everyone, but sometimes, two heads really are better than one!

Things like choosing a co-author, drawing up agreements about rights, etc., aren't what this book is about, so I won't go off on that particular tangent. Do make sure you have something ahead of time, including what happens to the rights if one of you dies, but again, that's beyond the scope of this book. Bottom line, if you and a trusted writer friend want to up your game and your word count, give some serious thought to co-writing.

What if it doesn't work out? What if we realize we're not compatible as co-writers? That's okay! I've had a number of false starts with people where we've wanted to write, but then either our voices didn't quite mesh or—more often than not—life happened and schedules went haywire. There's nothing wrong with tapping out.

Recommendations:

- Try co-writing to increase both enthusiasm and writing speed.
- Patience and grace—we all have lives outside of writing, and those lives can and do interfere sometimes.

CRUISE CONTROL

FINDING A COMFORTABLE, SUSTAINABLE SPEED

Because no two writers are alike, I can't tell you what your optimal writing speed would be. I can, however, help you figure out what that speed is. Or rather, what it should be.

I find that the best way to keep myself on task and get the most out of every writing session is to have a word count quota. More on how I track those in a little while, but before we get to that, let's talk about how to figure out what your quota should be.

First, figure out how much time you're going to devote each day or week to writing. Maybe you're going to set aside an hour every day. Or maybe two hours every Monday or Wednesday evening. Or all day Saturday. Whatever you can realistically devote in the long run. (And don't get discouraged if short, sporadic pockets of time are all you have available to you—if you take advantage of those pockets, the words will add up!)

Now, use that time for a week or so. However long it takes for you to have five to ten writing sessions. Keep track of how many words you write each session. Don't push yourself to write as much as possible—just write, and at the end, jot down the number along with how long you wrote.

See if a pattern emerges. If you're seeing roughly the same output per session (give or take 10%), then that's probably an easy, doable amount for you. If your numbers are all over the place, that's okay too. The more you do this, the more you'll see how much you can comfortably write per session. This is simply meant to give you a baseline—what you can produce without really breaking a sweat.

Now take a couple of writing sessions and push yourself. *Hard.* Try to double your output. If you can, try to triple it. Make every minute count, and pound that keyboard until your session is up.

Chances are, your word count will be much higher. However, you're not going to be able to sustain that kind of output for every session over the long term, and I wouldn't recommend trying unless you want to know what burnout feels like.

Things I learned the hard way so you don't have to: *Burnout sucks.*

So now you know how much you can write if you really, really push it, and how much you can write with minimal effort. Your magic number is somewhere in between. It's up to you to decide exactly where. It should be an amount that you can realistically write every session without burning yourself out, but also without just skating by.

As an example, I'll give you the numbers I use. Before I do, let me reiterate that I am a full-time writer, so my writing sessions are quite long (usually at least five or six hours). If I had only a couple of hours a day for writing, or kids or a day job to zap my energy, these numbers would understandably be much smaller.

If I plod through an six-hour session without really trying, I can easily write about 3,000 words. If I put the pedal to the floor and push myself, I can break 10,000. I don't want to write just the bare minimum, but I know I can't sustain the maximum speed for more than a few days in a row. With those numbers in mind, I came to a daily quota of 5,000 words. I have good days and bad days, of course, but whenever I sit down at my computer in the morning, I do so with the intent of writing 5,000 words. For me, that's sustainable enough that I've been doing it for the past fifteen years.

Does this mean you should never aim for your higher benchmark? Of course not! If you hit your quota early, and you feel ambitious, go for it! I push for 10,000 words every so often, even 15,000 if I'm really ambitious, and it's not unusual to hit 6,000 or 7,000 without collapsing.

This is where NaNoWriMo really helped me the most: With daily goals. By the time I was finished with NaNo in 2008, I had fallen into a rhythm of aiming for specific word counts every day. Before long, I had a spreadsheet that calculated how much I'd written that day and how much I had left to meet my goal.

That's not to say word counts are the end all, be all of writing. Of course quality is more important quantity. BUT... when I'm trudging along and hit one of those "I could call it a day" moments, and I see on my spreadsheet that I'm *almost* to the next 1,000 or 500 milestone, it's enough motivation to keep me writing until I hit that milestone. And more often than not, whatever I've written to hit that milestone is enough to give me a second (or third, or fourth) wind, which gets me almost to the next milestone, and so on. It can mean the difference between a 900 word day and a 5,000 word day.

Basically, you set the cruise control for your quota, and adjust as needed. Maybe you're on a roll, and the day is the equivalent of a long straight stretch with a tail wind. Turn off the cruise control and go! Or maybe it's a mountain pass day or an icy road day—forward motion is going to happen, but it's going to be slower and it's going to take more work. That's okay. Just be honest with yourself. Is it really a slow day? Or is it a lazy day?

And more to the point, have you had too many lazy days recently? Only one way to find out...

TRACKING YOUR WORDS

This brings me to what I mentioned earlier about keeping track of your daily output. I want to mention upfront that I do this in part because I do have some moderate ADHD and OCD, and the tracking helps to appease both. You play the hand you've been dealt, and this method works with my particular flavor of neurodivergence. As such, my tracking may be a bit stricter and more detailed than you require.

The other reasons, which may be useful to you:

1. To watch for patterns that might be indicative of burnout.
2. To push myself on days when I don't wanna.

The second one is pretty straightforward. I apparently have a high school gym teacher or a military drill instructor living in my head, and being able to look at my numbers gives that teacher-drill-sergeant dude ammo so he can scream "Are you really going to slack off today? You did 5,000 words every day this week, and now you're going to break that perfect streak with a piddly 2,000? Really?

REALLY? DROP AND GIVE ME ANOTHER THREE THOUSAND[1]."

My spreadsheet is also color-coded. After three "green" (5K) days in a row, the prospect of a yellow (2-3K) day messing up my pretty spreadsheet is enough to send me back to my Word document. It sounds silly, but believe me, that little bit of motivation—not wanting what amounts to a black mark on an otherwise pristine track record—can keep those words coming.

When I wrote this originally, I was coming up on four straight months of green days (not counting days off and editing days), and I said I wasn't ready to break that streak yet. Case in point: it's now 2023, fully *eight years later*, and that streak is *still holding*. Every writing day—non-editing, not a day off—has been green.

Let's say that wasn't the case, though, and I didn't have all greens. Much like a bunch of greens indicates a solidly productive period, if I've been lazy for a few days, it'll show in the form of lots of yellow or pink/salmon days but not many greens. That's usually more than enough to make me pull myself up by the bootstraps and put down some words.

But not every day *wants* to be a writing day. When I have a day where I just can't think, and I don't want to write, and I feel like the blinking cursor is going to be in my nightmares again, I look at my daily output spreadsheet. More often than not, the answer is pretty clear: a long stretch of days with solid outputs, but a serious lack of blank gray squares.

In other words: I haven't taken a day off in too long.

Burnout, y'all. The struggle is real.

So, let's talk about how I track my words. Before I show you my daily output spreadsheet, here is the color coding:

10,000+	
5,000-9,999	
3,001-4,999	
1,001-3,000	
<1,000	
day off	
Editing	

With that in mind, here is the daily output sheet:

Date	Words	Date	Words
2/8/2014	5,083	3/6/2014	5,762
2/9/2014	5,022	3/9/2014	
2/10/2014		3/10/2014	
2/11/2014	7,008	3/11/2014	5,891
2/12/2014		3/12/2014	5,395
2/13/2014	7,013	3/13/2014	5,068
2/14/2014		3/14/2014	
2/15/2014	5,048	3/15/2014	
2/16/2014	6,160	3/16/2014	6,000
2/17/2014	5,004	3/17/2014	5,004
2/18/2014		3/18/2014	
2/19/2014		3/19/2014	5,039
2/20/2014		3/20/2014	5,156
2/21/2014	10,121	3/21/2014	5,021
2/22/2014	5,081	3/22/2014	6,671
2/23/2014		3/23/2014	
2/24/2014	5,012	3/24/2014	6,209
2/25/2014	5,267	3/25/2014	2,038
2/26/2014	5,091	3/26/2014	2,463
2/27/2014	5,051	3/27/2014	
2/28/2014	5,241	3/28/2014	

The red triangles are where I've inserted comments to remind me of specific things. For example, March 25th is green even though I only wrote 2,038 words. This is because I finished my book that day, and whenever I finish something, it counts as a green day. In other places, such as March 26th, which is light blue to indicate I was editing that day, I inserted a comment to note which book I was working on.

I also keep track of how much I've written per month. I actually have several spreadsheets going that track word counts, progress, etc., but those won't necessarily be useful to you. How much you wish to track, whether or not you color code it or include comments... that's all up to you. My system has evolved over the last few years until it's exactly what I need; feel free to use it as a template if you wish, or create your own.

Even if you choose not to keep in-depth records like I do, I do recommend tracking your daily (or per session) output, at least as you find your groove. Your inner gym teacher may be able to use it to urge you to write more when you're thinking about calling it an early day. You'll be able to see patterns, especially periods where you're not writing as much as you need to be or—more importantly—when you're careening toward burnout.

Between establishing a quota for every writing session, and keeping track of when you meet that quota, you now have two more tools for disciplining yourself to write more every time you sit down at the keyboard.

Recommendations:

- Find a comfortable, sustainable writing speed.
- Track your output.
- If you would like a blank spreadsheet template like the one I use, please feel free to e-mail me at gallagherwitt@gmail.com

OUTLINING

LEAVING YOUR ENGLISH TEACHER BEHIND

This is not a book about outlines, but I think it's worthwhile to spend a little time talking about them. Why? Because for many writers, the key to writing faster is planning. I find it helps me write faster because instead of getting on a roll, writing like the wind, and then screeching to a halt and stalling, I can keep moving because I already figured out where I'm going. Even if it's just a vague concept or a few notes jotted down, direction and planning are your friends.

So, let's talk about outlines.

I know that word is enough to make some authors break out in hives or have flashbacks to high school English. This is because high school is a powerful thing that can turn Shakespeare into something as exciting as dried peanut butter and reduce the World War II to a dull landscape of names and dates.

With that in mind, let's start by evicting everything high school ever taught us about outlines. I hereby grant each and every one of you permission to forget everything your English teacher beat into you about outlines. There are no rules. There are no requirements. You don't have to use letters, followed by numbers, followed by Roman numerals, followed by...you get the idea.

You can use bullets or numbers or letters. It can be handwritten, typed, Morse code, whatever. Some people use whiteboards, spreadsheets, butcher paper on walls, or spiral notebooks. You can paint your outline on the side of a government building in red spray paint if that's what floats your boat[1].

Remember that your outline serves *you*. Therefore, it should be written, formatted, and adhered to only inasmuch as it helps you, the author, write your story. If you work best with a strict, detailed outline, then that's your style. If you work best with something vague and brief, there you go.

There are a number of resources out there that can offer tips and pointers on the specifics of outlining. My good friend Libbie Hawker's book *Take Off Your Pants!: Outline Your Books For Faster Writing* is not only hilariously titled, but offers an interesting, thorough, and useful outlining technique specifically designed to make drafting a book faster and more efficient. Try hers, try others, and eventually you'll find—or develop—the one that works best for you. My own method is a mishmash of things I've learned from other writers, including Libbie's method, that probably wouldn't work for anyone else but is exactly what I need. With time, you too will develop your own method.

But... what if an outline stifles your creativity?

I've heard a few writers say that once they've outlined, they have no interest in telling the story anymore because they've already told it. To this I say, think of your story as a joke. The outline is you hearing the joke yourself. The book is you telling the joke to your friend. You already know the punchline, but the excitement comes from sharing it with someone else so they can enjoy it the way you did.

To look at it another way, I am what you would call a tattoo enthusiast. Occasionally, I run into people who believe their artists are superior because they don't use stencils[2], and instead tattoo freehand. While I admire those who can freehand tattoo, I'm personally more comfortable with someone who will put the lines on my skin first, letting me make sure it really does look as good on my arm as it did on paper, that it's not crooked, etc., and the guidelines will keep him from drawing one of those lines that he'd have erased if he'd drawn on paper. Or, say, misspelling a word.

Things I learned the hard way so you don't have to: *If a tattoo is misspelled, too bad. Tattoo guns don't have erasers.*

Does it mean the artist is reduced to tracing lines, that the creativity is over and now it's just the drudgework of following lines he's already drawn? Of course not. Once the lines are in place, it's time to add color. More than once, upon finishing the outline of a tattoo, one of my artists has said "You know, now that I look at it, I think it would be really cool if we…"

Like the tattoo stencil, the outline doesn't keep the writer from being able to spread their creative wings—it simply ensures that you know whether you're drawing a mermaid or a shark before you start adding scales that you'll just end up removing later.

You also do not have to *stick* with your outline. Unlike a tattoo, outlines are changeable, and I promise that if you deviate from your outline, no one is going to flunk you or leave snide comments in the margins. I do it all the time—I'm a vague, flexible outliner who rarely writes exactly what I've outlined. For me, it's a guide, not a commitment, despite what was hammered into my head in school. The idea that an outline is unchangeable was on that would ultimately cause me years of pointless frustration. Once I'd decreed something, and it had taken its place beside the numeral or the letter or whatever, it could not be changed.

After far too many years of trying to shoehorn far too many scenes, stories, and characters into outlines, well...

Things I've learned the hard way so you don't have to: *Outlines are not written in blood.*

Also, if there is one rule that has never, ever led me astray in my writing career, it is this:

> If the characters and outline disagree,
> the characters *always* win.

15 years. Close to 200 titles. I have *always* followed that rule, and it has *never* failed me.

So how do I outline? Simply, vaguely, and flexibly. For me, the outline is mostly a means of keeping track of the *order* of events because I write out of sequence. Do the characters meet before the Corvette incident, but after the fishing trip? Awesome. Now I know whether or not they can make comments about the rabid bass they caught, or if the love interest already has the imprint on his forehead from the Corvette symbol. So basically, the outline helps me keep the story's chronology straight so I can write out of sequence without creating continuity errors.

I use an Excel spreadsheet for reasons that will be clear later in the book (see the sections on writing out of sequence and bite-sized writing). Each chapter gets a one-line summary so I remember what's supposed to happen there.

Some scenes can be as simple as "They meet." Notice how there's nothing indicating where, how, why, or if there's a malfunctioning cotton candy machine involved, only that the characters meet. That's because my outline is not there to dictate every detail of the scene, only when it happens in relation to other scenes.

Other scenes will, of course, require more explanation:

"They break up because she found out he still lives with his mother[3]."

"Jude can't stop thinking about A.J.; pulls him aside after the show to talk about what happened."

"Kristine finds the book; discovers Ryan has been lying. Calls Det. Johnson."

I give it as much detail as it needs, but that usually isn't much, and the beauty of that is that it gives me complete freedom for twists, turns, and surprises. For example, in the third "chapter" above, where Kristine finds the book and calls the detective, she might also find some other tidbits in Ryan's apartment that offer more clues about his character or the story that even I didn't know about—a copy of his estranged father's will, a set of keys with a make/model that is way out of his price range, or a jacket that is far too small for him.

So what happens if one of those tidbits has the potential to alter the course of the story? Run with it! Just because the story is outlined doesn't mean you can't surprise yourself!

Speaking of which, I mentioned earlier that I write out of sequence and frequently change my outlines. If I find myself working on a scene in chapter 13 that illuminates a fatal error with chapter 4, I run with it and change chapter 4. If chapter 7 actually needs to come after chapter 17, I rearrange, renumber, and continue.

And to reiterate:

> If the characters and outline disagree,
> the characters *always* win.

So basically...

1. Have an outline or at least a vague plan,
   especially if you want to write out of order,
   unless you're one of those human-alien hybrids
   who can do that on the fly.
2. Let thy characters guide you.

How detailed should your outline be? That's your call. How much information do you need? I've heard many writers ask, "Do I need more than this for an outline? Have I outlined enough? Is anything missing?"

The answer to that is... you tell me. For my own outlines, all I need to know is what happens in the scene and why. And it can be very vague.

When I'm writing a romance, scenes can be simply:

- Characters meet.
- Love interest reveals something from his past that doesn't sit well with the other character.
- Characters break up because of X, Y, or Z.

Or for a suspense novel:

- Detective arrives at murder scene; discovers knife and bloody glass.
- Woman calls, says she is connected to victim. When detective goes to meet her, she turns up dead.

You get the idea. You only need to outline as much information as *you need* in order to write the story. For me, I just need enough to know the basic sequence of events. If I'm writing an interrogation scene, I need to know if it's happening before or after the detective met the suspect's wife because that'll tell me whether or not the detective needs to ask the suspect about a particular comment she made.

Things I learned the hard way so you don't have to: *Outlining is not writing. No matter how many times and in how much detail you write your outline, you still have to eventually sit down and write the book. ...she said after endlessly tweaking an outline for ten years before finally writing the stupid thing.*

Outlines—how they're set up, if they're used at all—are very much individualized. There is no right or wrong way. For the purpose of this book, I encourage outlining because I'm going to discuss some methods that work better (at least for me) if there's an outline in place.

Even if outlining absolutely doesn't work for you, I recommend that when you sit down to write, you have some kind of plan. Cari and I don't outline when we co-write, but we usually know in general terms what's going to happen in the next few scenes. Half the time, we're wrong, and somebody throws a giant curve ball that neither of us saw coming, and that's okay! The point is that when we sit down to write, we have at least an idea of where we think we're going.

It's kind of like deciding to go out for a drive. It's a lot more fun to jump in the car and *go* than it is to sit in the driveway debating whether to go right or left. You don't have to have a destination in mind, but it helps to at least have a direction. Then you can get in the car, get on the freeway, and put the pedal to the floor, and if something looks interesting along the way, stop and check it out.

By the same token...

...don't plan things to death. In my fledgling writer days, I wrote that horrible epic fantasy novel three times over the course of about ten years. Each actual draft took about 4-6 months, depending on what else I had going on in my life. So why did it take ten years? Well, a lot of that had to do with getting derailed and sidetracked with other things like jobs and school, but there were some very long periods in there where I *planned*. And planned. And planned. I outlined. Re-outlined. Built the world. Drew maps. Outlined again. Burned the world to the ground and started over. Filled out countless character inter-views/forms/dossiers/bios. For every hour I spent writing that bad boy, I probably spent at least twenty planning it. (And it still sucked. Go figure.)

The cold hard truth is that at some point, you have to put down the blueprint and start building the damned house. You can measure and re-measure every angle and beam, but you'll still have nothing but an empty lot until you actually start pouring some concrete and building the frame.

Be flexible. As a vague outliner, I know what the charac-ters' motivations are, what they're going to do and why, and when things will happen. But invariably, those things change. Constantly. The rigid outliner in me—you know, the one who's never forgotten high school English—still wants to break out in hives at the idea of deviating from the outline that's been written in blood, carved in stone, and notarized twelve times over. But the side of me who's always rebelled against my high school English teachers and doesn't like to be told what to do has no qualms about adjusting an outline to fit the story.

How does that help with writing at speed? It prevents three things:

1. Time and energy wasted trying to shoehorn a story into an outline it doesn't like.
2. Time and energy wasted rejigging the outline down to the last detail because the story rebelled.
3. Time and energy wasted expanding the outline because there is always, always, always some other angle or detail it can include.

Common denominators: wasting time and energy.

If the story deviates from the outline, go with it. This is kind of like improv. If another actor throws a monkey wrench into the scene in front of a packed house, do you stop in the middle and ask him what he thinks he's doing? Or do you take his cue and run with it? Of course you run with it. In writing, if a character throws me a curve ball, chances are, he knows what he's doing, so I let the scene go and see what happens.

Now, a little bit of a tangent here about writing in general, which may or may not help you with writing speed, but feels relevant...

One thing that always comes up on writing forums is the idea of characters hijacking the story. Some writers insist that it's true, that characters are basically living entities who can't be controlled, and the author is just along for the ride. Others think it's utter hogwash and *they* are in control of everything. Personally, I think the truth lies somewhere in the middle.

Imagine someone you know really, really well. You know their quirks, their history, their morals, their preferences, etc. Now imagine writing them into a story. Think of something that person absolutely would not do under any circumstances. Let's say Grandma would never in a million years steal a wrench from the hardware store. Not a chance. With that in mind, try writing a scene where she's going just that, and she's feeling completely justified about it and not considering any alternatives.

Doesn't work, does it?

Characters are the same way. They are a collection of quirks, traits, and morals, and at least in my experience, sometimes those quirks, traits, and morals become clearer as I'm writing the story (versus when I wrote the outline). Then I find them in a position where I'm asking them to do what the outline says, but I just can't get the words to come out. I thought I knew how this character would behave, but then I got to the scene and realized there's no way I'm going to make Grandma steal that wrench. But she still needs the wrench, right? Instead of forcing her to do what the outlines said, it's time to rethink the scene according to Grandma's quirks, traits, and morals, and how she—your 3-dimensional character—would acquire the wrench.

What does *that* have to do with writing speed? Well, allowing some flexibility and giving your characters room to come to life means the story has some breathing room to flow and do its thing, while Rigid Outliner is banging on the Backspace key trying to figure out how to make Grandma steal the goddamned wrench already.

So...don't stall out. Let her find another way to get her hands on the wrench. She'll be truer to her character, will probably come up with a more interesting way to acquire it, and...you'll be writing instead of stalling.

And if you need the reminder, my recommendation for the end of this chapter is to tape this above your writing space where you can always see it:

**If the outline and the characters disagree,
the characters *always* win.**

WRITING OUT OF SEQUENCE

This technique is definitely a key to my writing speed.

In the beginning, I wrote chronologically like most sane, reasonable people, but at some point, during my early writing days, I started writing out of sequence.

It started innocently enough. I'd be clipping along with my story, but an upcoming scene would bother me. It would refuse to let me sleep, and I'd obsess over it, itching to get to it so I could finally write it.

I found myself doing one of two things:

- Completely stalling because I was too distracted by a later scene to write the scenes before it.
- Rushing through the scenes to get to the one I wanted to write.

I wasn't above rushing through scenes to get to the one I really wanted to write. And yeah, it worked out about as well as it sounds. Instead of beating my head against a wall to get through the stubborn scene, I skipped ahead and worked on something else...like, for example, the one that wouldn't shut up.

So finally, I decided to just write the scene and get it out of my system, then go back to the scenes before it. It worked beautifully. With that scene written and squared away, I could focus on the preceding scenes and not rush them or feel bogged down by them.

Over time, this madness evolved until my only inclination to write even remotely chronologically was to start with Chapter 1. I still do that. After about 100 words, I'll probably flit over to Chapter 17 for a little while. These days, it's a rare occasion when I write a *paragraph* in order. This entire book? All over the place.

Bonus? It's not unusual at all for the stubborn scenes to get unstuck after I've written a later scene. Maybe I'm just not in the mood to write a car chase scene today. Maybe I really don't feel like writing a sex scene. Maybe I need to write that emotional breakdown scene before it keeps me up for another night.

But... how does it work?

Well, think of your outline the way filmmakers think of a storyboard—it's a visual representative of the story and how it's going to play out, but the scenes are not *filmed* in chronological order. And that's what you're doing here —"filming" your story.

Remember, there are no rules about how you have to get it done, as long as you do get it done.

Let's start with a little bit on *how* to write out of sequence, and then I'll get to more about why, advantages/disadvantages, Batman, etc. Yes, Batman's involved.

How to Write Out of Sequence

So how does it work, anyway?

As with anything, there's no one way to do this. If there was, that would mean this was a sane, reasonable technique employed by sane, reasonable people, but it's not. So, I'll offer tips and pointers based on how I do it, but please take them all with an entire mine full of salt. Should you try any of them and find they are disastrous on an "invade Russia in the winter" level, then by all means, reject them.

Okay, we all know what's coming. I know this is going to make a few people hit the brakes and yell "NOPE!", but hear me out, y'all.

Even if you've dug your heels in since the chapter on outlining and are valiantly holding out against the idea, **you'll probably want to at least *consider* outlining** at this stage. I know some authors do this without an outline, but I have no idea how they manage it, and if I tried, my brain would melt out of my left nostril. In the interest of keeping brain matter out of my sinuses, which have already been mercilessly ravaged by three brutal Nebraska winters, I'm going to let those people do their thing while I do mine.

So henceforth, I'm going to assume you're onboard with outlining.

Precisely how out of sequence you write is entirely up to you. Some people write entire scenes. Some people write a few paragraphs here and there, and eventually sew them all together into a cohesive scene. Me, I'm all over the place. I usually have at least 300-500 words in every chapter of a book before I ever *finish* one chapter. Then I'll just add 100 or so here and there—and sometimes go off on a tear and blow through one scene all at once—and before I know it, the book is done.

The biggest thing is just to keep yourself organized

enough to know what to write and where, but not so strictly outlined/planned that you suffocate yourself. I know, that doesn't sound terribly helpful. "Just do what you want and try not to get lost." But that's pretty much what it boils down to.

Okay, but why? It sounds kind of complicated.

So...

What are some of the advantages of writing out of sequence?

I mentioned a couple of pros and cons earlier. There's also preventing continuity errors, ridiculously easy fore-shadowing, etc. A couple of things I'd particularly like to highlight in this section:

1. Some scenes are a pain in the butt to write.
2. Some books are a pain in the butt to finish.

Let's face it: Even the easiest book that's just rocking its way out of your head via your fingers is going to have its moments. It's kind of like being on a road trip with awesome friends and Batman. You're flying down the interstate, having the time of your life with your friends and Batman, listening to the radio and Batman's stories and totally not questioning a) why you haven't seen a cop for the last 100 miles or b) why Batman's even hanging out with you, but...

...sooner or later, someone will have to stop and pee. I'm not naming names or necessarily saying Batman's the one who's gotta pee, but one way or another, you're eventually going to have to start watching for a gas station or rest stop, slow down, pull into a parking space, and come down from your high-while-sober euphoria of fun to peruse a dirty convenience store's snack aisle while you wait for Batman to come out of the bathroom. Then it's back on the road for more fun and Batman.

Which is an incredibly long and belabored way of saying...sometimes you will stall or hit a not-so-fun-to-write part of the book. Sometimes there's a scene you just don't feel like writing. I've argued many times with people who think that if a scene is difficult or troublesome to write, it's probably going to be difficult or troublesome to read. If I don't feel like writing it, the reader won't feel like reading it. I disagree. Honestly, every single one of my books has at least one scene that I beat my head against before it finally came together. There are some scenes that were so difficult to write for whatever reason, I would literally add two or three sentences, then go work on something else.

The thing is, not every exciting-to-read scene is exciting to write. And sometimes, in order to get from one exciting-to-write scene to another, you need another scene in between that is necessary and interesting to *read*, but for whatever reason, excruciating to *write*. Writing that scene is the Batman pee break of the road trip: like it or not, it's gotta happen.

For me, the Batman pee breaks are usually sex scenes and car chases. Car chases are seriously the bane of my existence, and for reasons I'll never fully understand, I find sex scenes incredibly difficult to write. But since I write erotic fiction, they are obviously necessary.

What in the name of all that's good and unholy does this have to do with writing out of sequence?

Everything, my dear friends. Everything. To a degree, this goes back to what I said earlier about jumping ahead to write a scene that you can't get out of your head, but it gets even better here.

Imagine, if you will, that you're on your road trip with Batman. Now imagine you're like fifty miles from Vegas, and you are itching to sit down at the baccarat table and out-baccarat James Bond. And a hundred miles after that, you're going to visit Area 51 and are guaranteed to witness an alien abduction.

What if you could teleport ahead, skip the miles of desert and the *OMG Batman seriously another freaking pee breaks*, and park yourself at the baccarat table? And once you were done with that, you could snap your fingers and be in your front row lawn chair at Area 51?

Guess what?

You totally can.

Skip ahead. Write the baccarat scene. Then skip ahead again and write the Area 51 scene. While you're at it, jump back to the pre-baccarat driving and write in a witty, foreshadowy snippet of dialogue that you hadn't thought of before. When those are done, time warp all the way to the end and write the wicked cool epilogue involving a reincarnated Joan of Arc and a disembodied owl brain.

See? Words are flying! The scenes are landing on paper, and they're awesome! A few more scenes, and you're done with this bad boy!

Which of course brings us back to Batman and his temperamental bladder.

Yes, we can skip around and write all the exciting-to-write scenes, and knock out all the scenes that just wanted to happen right now, but sooner or later, you're gonna have to suck it up, pull into a rest stop, and let the dude do his business.

In my case, this usually means going back and writing at least one or two of the sex scenes, or going back and finally finishing that car chase which is currently nothing more than a dozen or so sentences scattered throughout an otherwise blank document[1].

So... really? Now we have to sit down and write the scenes that are really hard to write? Now that all the cool scenes are done?

Yes. But look at it this way: those scenes are the only thing standing between you and *a finished book*.

Let me give you an example. I was wrapping up *Razor Wire*, one of my military romances. That book had been flyyyying out of my fingertips, words hitting the page like... like... okay, let's just let this one go before I find a way to bring it back to Batman stopping and peeing again. Point being, *Razor Wire* was flying.

Except for the second sex scene. I was flitting all over the book, adding 100 words here and 500 there, but every time I came to that scene...crickets.

I couldn't take the scene out because it was necessary for the story. There was nothing wrong with the scene, I just...didn't feel like writing it. It was that simple. Sort of like the car chase scene in *The Given & The Taken*. It was absolutely necessary to the story, and when it was finished, my betas were thrilled with it. They also couldn't tell that writing it was word dentistry.

With both the car chase in *The Given & The Taken*, and the sex scene in *Razor Wire*, I eventually found myself in the same situation: the entire book was written except for *that scene*. That one, troublesome scene that had to happen.

Now, it was still a struggle to finish those scenes, but it made a huge difference knowing that once they were finished, *the book would be finished*. It was decidedly less daunting to approach those scenes knowing I'd be done with the entire manuscript, rather than "Okay, now on to the next 50,000 words..."

Bottom line:

1. Writing out of sequence allows you to write the scenes that your brain wants to write without a) blowing through the less interesting ones just to get to the good ones, or b) completely stalling out because you can't get past the less interesting ones.
2. Writing out of sequence can also put you in a position where the less interesting scene is the only thing standing between you and a finished book.

A couple of points about that:

1. To reiterate, when I say "less interesting" scenes, I don't mean less interesting to read. Some scenes are just tougher to write, or aren't as exciting to write, but are still mission critical and absolutely interesting to read. Make sure you know the difference. Is this scene just tough to write? Or is your reluctance/difficulty a sign that there's a problem with the scene? Does Batman really have to pee, or is he just being a jerk?
2. For some people, writing all the exciting stuff first can backfire. There's nothing left but the hard scenes, so... meh. Why bother? For me, it's like chapter peer pressure. All the other chapters are done, and they're glaring at chapters 15 and 23 like "WTF, dude? Get your head out of your butt," and that's enough to

motivate me to pound out those chapters. Know
thy mind, know thy limits.

As with anything, if a technique or explanation doesn't
work for you, toss it aside and ignore it. Part of this game is
figuring out what works, and there is no 'one size fits all' on
this particular rack.

So now everything is set up, you've planned as much as
you need to plan, it's time to write...out of sequence!

First things first:

Don't Be Afraid to Write *Way* Out of Sequence.

I don't just mean writing chapters out of order, my friends.
As I've mentioned previously, I write *paragraphs* out of
order. I'm not kidding. I'll write a few sentences here, a few
paragraphs there, and eventually they come together in a
cohesive scene, which becomes a cohesive chapter, which
eventually joins forces with the other chapters to create a
manuscript that's like the bastard lovechild of Franken-
stein's Monster and Voltron.

Doesn't that make for an editing nightmare, though?
Believe it or not, it really doesn't. I actually found I had
more continuity errors and such when I tried to write in
sequence than when I started writing out of sequence.
Why? Because as I flit back and forth between chapters, I
can make minor adjustments to keep the continuity going.

For example, let's say you're happily working on your story
when your character needs to, at a most inopportune moment,
have an allergic reaction to something. Let's say he's terribly
allergic to artificial sweeteners. You're working on chapter 19,

and your character orders a Coke, but the waiter accidentally gives him a Diet Coke. (Yes, I know, this is a ridiculous example, but I'm just making a point) And you stop and ask yourself, "Have I mentioned this anywhere else in the book? Uh oh."

Fortunately, that restaurant scene in chapter 11 isn't finished, and neither is a conversation with his co-worker in chapter 5. Which means it's now simple to scoot back to one —or even both—of those chapters, and write a little snippet that will foreshadow his NutraSweet allergy. Maybe his co-worker offers him some sort of healthy snack, and he cautiously asks if it has any artificial sweeteners in it. Then in the restaurant scene, his date puts Equal into her iced tea, and he suddenly realizes he can't remember which glass is his and which is hers, so he asks, adding a casual, "Just checking. I'm allergic to NutraSweet."

Obviously that's a ridiculous example, but you get the idea. The point is, if you see something that needs foreshadowing, it's very easy to go back to other chapters and slip in that foreshadowing without having to rewrite, reorganize, or whatever.

And by the same token, sometimes later chapters reveal things you didn't know about earlier ones. When I was working on *All The King's Horses*, I was having a lot of trouble with the beginning and the ending because I couldn't see the characters' motivations as clearly as I needed to. I did have a pretty solid grasp on some of the chapters in the middle, though, so I decided to write those. In doing so, letting the characters do what was in character for them, I actually figured out that I had the beginning all wrong and the ending needed a massive overhaul. By the time chapters 9-13 were finished, I finally understood what needed to happen in the preceding *and* following chapters.

Instead of getting stuck and stalling out, I skipped ahead, and stumbled across the solution.

So don't be afraid to try bouncing around within your manuscript. Writing out of sequence can save you time and frustration, and keep you from stalling over a troublesome scene. And of course, when you aren't frustrated and you aren't stalling, you'll be more productive.

But what about those days when you'd rather eat glass than write at all? Well, if writing out of sequence works for you, then I have a solution for those days as well...

BITE-SIZED WRITING

Once I got the hang of writing out of order, this technique was kind of a natural progression. This is how I get the words out on days when I wake up with a great big lump of Don't Wanna where my brain used to be. Even though I love writing, there are times when I just... don't... *wanna*.

Staring down a 5,000-word quota on a day like that is enough to make me want to crawl under my desk and suck my thumb. Or clean my house. That's when you know it's not a good day.

But you know what? Sometimes the Don't Wanna days can actually turn into solid productive days, and there is a certain feeling of satisfaction that comes from hitting the day's quota when I started out thinking I wouldn't break 500.

Things I've learned the hard way so you don't have to: *Sometimes a "Don't Wanna" day is actually a sign of burnout. Listen to your body and your mind.*

With that out of the way, the technique that helps me get past the Great Wall of Don't Wanna and conquer my quota involves breaking the writing up into little tiny bite-sized pieces. For this technique, it does help to have a way of keeping track of your word counts per chapter. If you don't utilize such a method, that's fine—just make a mental note of the word count when you begin your chapter, and when you've reached your goal.

So here's how it works. Let's say your book has twenty-five chapters. You've outlined it enough to know what goes on in each of those chapters.

Now, let's also say that the Don't Wanna in your skull doesn't like the idea of writing 2,500 words, but it can grudgingly allow you to write 100.

Open up chapter 1. Write 100 words.

Open up chapter 2. Write 100 words.

Do this all the way through, and you've got 2,500 words written. Bam. That easy.

No, seriously. It's that easy. All you have to do is muster up the energy to write one hundred words. This paragraph? The one you're reading now? Exactly fifty words. If you can write two paragraphs like this in every chapter of your twenty-five chapter book, you've written 2,500 words.

If you're really struggling, make it fifty words. If you want to push, make it 200. The whole point is that you're breaking up your session's word count goal into little morsels of text, which I personally find a lot less daunting than staring down the barrel of 5,000.

Now, what happens if you're writing your 100 words, but you start picking up speed and you're on a roll? Keep going! The whole idea is to get your fingers moving and the words flowing. For me, the result of this is very frequently the same: after three or four chapters of writing a tidbit here and there, one paragraph will turn into two, and that'll turn into ten, and the next thing I know, I've written over 1,000 words without blinking.

While I was writing *The Virgin Cowboy Billionaire's Secret Baby* (yes, that really is the title), I had a Don't Wanna day, but I decided for whatever reason that I could handle writing some setting details in each chapter. Yeah, I don't know either, but I was on a deadline, so I ran with it.

This came from a chapter where my character who has just moved back to her hometown after ten years away is attending the local rodeo:

> *As she neared the arena, the other familiar smells reached her, like distant faces coming into focus. Dust, horses, hay, and cedar shavings, not to mention overcooked hot dogs and stale popcorn coming from the concession stand, were overwhelming but it was nostalgia more than nausea.*
>
> *Like the Coolidge farm, the fairgrounds were simultaneously different and the same as they'd been since she was a kid. The arena had the same old concession stand, and she was pretty sure the two line cooks had been there way back then, along with some of the burgers and pretzels now that she thought about it.*

That right there? 103 words.

In another chapter, the same character is visiting an old friend. So, I opened up the document to write 100 words of setting details:

Funny—even if she'd just walked in here off the street without knowing who lived here, she'd have guessed in an instant that it was Matt's house. He'd always had two or three video game consoles, though back then, they'd been dusty secondhand systems in a particle board TV stand from Wal-Mart. The particle board would've been straining beneath one of those TVs that had a crappy medium-sized screen, but still weighed five hundred pounds.

Those days were over. Now he had a slick flat screen—probably one of those ultra high definition ones where you could see the fleas on the dogs in the background—and only the latest and greatest video game technology. He had both an Xbox 360 and an Xbox 1, and both a PS3 and a PS4. Just like she did. She suspected that if she looked through the neat stacks of games flanking the entertainment center that she'd find quite a few familiar titles.

She smiled to herself. Some things never changed.

168 words. Notice how it ends up adding more than just scenery, but also hints about the characters.

So then, even with a head full of Don't Wanna, I've managed 271 words in two chapters.

Approach it however you want to. Maybe you're just going to write dialogue. Maybe setting details. Maybe little snippets of the scenes as they come to you. It doesn't matter —the only thing that matters is that even though you didn't feel like it, *you're writing.*

How you keep track of that is up to you. I've used scratch paper, or you could mentally track it—whatever works. I use a spreadsheet, of course—I modify my Excel-based outline to show how much I want to write in each chapter that day. If you'd like a copy of that spreadsheet and instructions on how to use it, you can always send me an e-mail (gallagherwitt@gmail.com) and request a copy of my template spreadsheet, which will have the columns and formulas already entered. I'm happy to share it with anyone who wants it, and you're welcome to change it however you see fit.

Does all of this sound ridiculous? Yes. Even I roll my eyes when I'm explaining it, because it sounds stupid. But I cannot tell you how many Don't Wanna days I have turned into good, solid, quota-meeting days. Not long ago, I was having an off week, and I did this four days in a row. Next thing I knew, I was 20,000 words farther into my book, and a good half dozen chapters were better than two-thirds finished. Sometimes, if I'm feeling ambitious, I'll even set the individual chapter quotas a bit higher, and knock out 10,000 words or more. Try it—*it works*.

And one final thing, something I cannot emphasize enough about using this particular technique:

Do. Not. Cheat.

You're not doing yourself any favors if you just write 100 words of garbage in each chapter. You still have to think about what you're writing. This isn't an exercise in barfing words onto the page—it's just a way to break up the large task (daily quota) into something that's not so daunting (individual chapter quota). No skipping the use of contractions, or leaving out hyphens, or naming every character Mary Sue or Captain Jack von Lotsawords, or throwing in some info dumps, just to up your quota. You only have to write 100 words, so there's no excuse not to *make them count*. Then move to the next chapter and make *those* 100 words count.

And before you know it, those 100 word nibbles will add up to more than you thought you'd write today.

AFTERWORD

IF YOU LISTEN TO ONE THING IN THIS BOOK, LET IT BE THIS.

So now you've hopefully learned a technique or two that will help you improve your speed and output. Over time, you'll likely adapt and bend those techniques until they're your own. I wish you the best of luck.

Before you close this book, however, let me offer some parting words in the form of a cautionary tale. Above all the advice and pointers I've given, nothing is more important than being vigilant of your mental and physical health. Writing at speed is fun, and it's productive, and it can get addictive. The exhilaration of finishing a book does diminish a little as you finish more and more of them, but there is still a high, a thrill. So too is there a thrill when a book is sold or released. And like speed, those can be addictive. You want it again, so you push yourself harder. Before long, by the time the rush of one finish or one release has faded, you're well on your way to the next one.

While it's well and good to ride your momentum, it can backfire rather spectacularly.

Think I'm kidding?

Things I learned the hard way so you don't have to: *Everything you're about to read.*

As I mentioned early on, I started writing full-time at the end of 2008. After finishing my first romance during NaNo-WriMo, I wanted to keep my momentum going, so I jumped into the next one. And the next one. And the next one.

By 2011, it had become a running joke that I was a workaholic. I would start writing early in the day, stop for dinner, and go back to it until nearly midnight. When this took a serious toll on my marriage, I adjusted my hours and started working 9-6, spending the evenings with my husband instead of my keyboard.

The workaholic thing didn't go away, though. Every so often, I would sit down to write, and find myself unable to conjure up the energy to do more than answer e-mails or play games on my iPad. A pattern emerged. When those days occurred, I checked my daily word count spreadsheet, and almost without fail, I'd be on day 18 or 19 without taking a day off. I started scheduling days off to avoid hitting that almost-three-week wall.

By 2012, though, I had regular deadlines. As soon as one book was finished, I had to dive right into the next one, or even work on two, three, or four simultaneously. This was fine—I enjoy working at that pace. Except sometimes the pace required me to ignore those scheduled days off. Still, it was manageable... most of the time.

The problems started in 2013. I was starting to get tired. I ended up taking a month off for a trip to Europe, which helped a lot, but when I returned, the deadlines were still there, as were the unfinished projects. Rested and refreshed, I jumped right back in.

In early 2014, I hit a breaking point. I needed to stop.

Unfortunately, I couldn't.

You see, the deadlines had begun to snowball. Burnout had been slowing me down, and as I crawled toward each deadline, they raced toward me, one after the other. Then I hurt my shoulder. Then some personal crises came up. I had to bow out of a conference at the last minute because I simply couldn't afford to take a week away from the computer and get farther behind. There was another conference coming up in just four weeks, and I had four novels that needed to be finished first.

I finished two of them. The second was finished on the plane en route to the conference. Right after the conference, I took another trip, but it was one where I still needed to write.

It was there that I hit the wall.

I opened my inbox to find yet another set of edits, and I just... couldn't. But I had to. The only way I'd be able to stop and relax was by finishing everything that was on my plate. The only way out, it seemed, was through.

Something had to give, though, and I took a few days off. Probably the longest stretch of not-writing and not-editing I'd had in a while. It helped, but I was still burned out. So, *so* burned out.

And the pile of work remained. The deadlines kept coming.

By now, it was June of 2014. Knowing I needed to get through everything before I could take a break, I pushed through as hard as I could. Ultimately, it took until the middle of August to catch up. As it happened, this was shortly after another large conference. My roommate was hit hard by the dreaded con crud, but I escaped.

Or so it seemed.

A couple of weeks after the conference, I finished one

last project, submitted it, and was free. There were dead-lines off in the distance, but they were spread apart now. I was, for the first time in two years, completely caught up, and I could take that break I'd so desperately needed.

And just like that, my immune system collapsed.

Within days of turning in that last project, I had walking pneumonia. Over the next four months, it would beat me down for two or three weeks at a time, recede, and then relapse a total of four times.

And those deadlines that were off in the distance? They were all up in my face now.

In the end, I pleaded with my publishers for extensions. Fortunately, no one argued. In fact, they'd been on my back for a while now to stop overworking myself, so they eagerly cancelled my deadlines and told me to recover, and then get the books done. Three months later, fully a year after I hit the wall and desperately needed to change something, I was finally on a reasonable, manageable, *sustainable* schedule.

And as I update this book now in 2023, fully nine years after that awful year, I am *still dealing* with long term health issues as a result. Burning myself out to the point my immune system collapsed resulted in problems that snow-balled and snowballed for years, culminating in some fairly major surgery in early 2022, from which I only completely recovered in early 2023.

Burnout is no joke, my friends.

The moral to this long and convoluted story is this—know your limits. Many writers live by the mantra "write every day," but we writerly creatures are only human. If you feel you need to take a day off, take one. If you feel like you've bitten off more than you can chew, do damage control before it starts causing problems.

Remember that even though writing is hard work, it

should still be enjoyable. One of the fastest routes to destroying that joy is writing yourself into the ground until you can barely function.

So while you've hopefully learned a thing or two that'll help you write more in less time, remember that with great power comes great responsibility. Your responsibility is to yourself, as well as to the people who'd like you to step away from your computer once in a while. You really, really, really don't have to suffer for your art. If you find that you are suffering, step away for a little while. Go spend some time with someone whose company you enjoy. Go to the beach. Go for a walk.

Downtime is not only okay for writers, it is essential. Even if your brain is always at least partly tuned in to your writing, the rest of it needs to disconnect sometimes. Your body, your mind, your writing, and the people around you will thank you. Trust me.

So go forth, writers.

Make words.

Make stories.

Make progress.

And for heaven's sake, take care of yourself.

RECOMMENDED READING & AUTHORS

These are books that helped me in my early days as a writer.

- *On Writing* by **Stephen King** – If ever there was a book that I thought should be required reading for fledgling writers, it's this one. Part autobiography, part discussion of Stephen King's writing techniques, it's a fantastic source of inspiration and motivation.
- *Writing the Breakout Novel* by **Donald Maass**
- *Take Off Your Pants! Outline Your Books For Faster Writing* by **Libbie Hawker**
- *Write Great Fiction: Characters, Emotion, & Viewpoint* by **Nancy Kress**
- **Plot & Structure** by **James Scott Bell**
- *How Not to Write a Novel: 200 Classic Mistakes and How to Avoid Them* by

Howard Mittelmark & Sandra Newman

I also encourage writers of every level to join the Absolute Write online community. There are thousands of writers on that forum, ranging from nervous novices to New York Times bestsellers.

The NaNoWriMo (National Novel Writing Month) online communities are mostly active in October and November, but some of the regional groups and such are active year-round.

Authors who were mentioned within the text:

Erica Cameron (my trusty beta reader for this book!)

Libbie Hawker (author of *Take Off Your Pants!: Outline Your Books For Faster Writing*)

Cari Z

Anna Zabo

K.A. Merikan

Marie Sexton

Aislinn Kerry

For more books by L.A. Witt, please visit

http://www.gallagherwitt.com

Romance * Suspense

Contemporary * Historical * Sports * Military

Titles Include

Rookie Mistake (written with Anna Zabo)

Scoreless Game (written with Anna Zabo)

The Hitman vs. Hitman Series (written with Cari Z)

The Bad Behavior Series (written with Cari Z)

The Gentlemen of the Emerald City Series

The Anchor Point Series

The Husband Gambit

Name From a Hat Trick

After December

Brick Walls

The Venetian and the Rum Runner

If The Seas Catch Fire

...and many, many more!

ABOUT THE AUTHOR

L.A. Witt is a romance and suspense author who has at last given up the exciting nomadic lifestyle of the military spouse (read: her husband finally retired). She now resides in Pittsburgh, where the potholes are determined to eat her car and her cats are endlessly taunted by a disrespectful squirrel named Moose. In her spare time, she can be found painting in her art room or destroying her voice at a Pittsburgh Penguins game.

Website: www.gallagherwitt.com
   Email: gallagherwitt@gmail.com
   Twitter: @GallagherWitt

NOTES

INTRODUCTION

1. If you are aware of an incantation that will render one immune to burnout, please let me know.

THIS SPACE IS YOUR SPACE

1. I recommend doing this at home, but it doesn't tend to go over very well in coffee shops.
2. I was not there for an actual funeral.

RESEARCH

1. This is not meant as a swipe against romances, or to imply they're somehow "less than" historical fiction and thrillers. I'm a romance author myself, so I'm not about to make that implication. Generally speaking, though, a contemporary romance will require less *research* than a suspense novel or historical fiction.

TRACKING YOUR WORDS

1. Yes, my internal drill sergeant/gym teacher is kind of a jerk.

OUTLINING

1. I don't actually recommend this. Please don't do it. And if you do, don't blame me. Though it would be kind of funny if something like that went viral—*Vandal Claims Author of Writing How-To Book Told Them To Spray Paint White House*. It *would* be funny, but would also be bad. So... don't do it. Please.
2. A tattoo stencil is basically a temporary tattoo that's used to make sure the design is in the right place, and the artist then traces the lines with the permanent ones.

3. For the record, none of my characters have ever broken up with other characters because someone lives at home with their mother.

WRITING OUT OF SEQUENCE

1. Car chase scenes are seriously going to be the literary (not literal!) death of me.